How to use this book

Follow the advice, in italics, where given.
Support the children as they read the text that is shaded in cream.
Praise *the children at every step!*
Detailed guidance is provided in the Read Write Inc. Phonics Handbook.
Activity 8 (Answer the 'questions to read and answer') only appears in Sets 4–7.

8 reading activities
Children:
1 *Practise reading the speed sounds.*
2 *Read the green and red words for the non-fiction text.*
3 *Listen as you read the introduction.*
4 *Discuss the vocabulary check with you.*
5 *Read the non-fiction text.*
6 *Re-read the non-fiction text and discuss the 'questions to talk about'.*
7 *Re-read the non-fiction text with fluency and expression.*
9 *Practise reading the speed words.*

Speed sounds

Consonants *Say the pure sounds (do not add 'uh').*

f	l	m	n	r	s	v	z	sh	th	ng
	ll						s			nk

b	c	d	g	h	j	p	qu	t	w	x	y	ch
	k											tch
	ck											

Vowels *Say the vowel sound and then the word, e.g. 'a', 'at'.*

at	hen	in	on	up	day	see	high	blow	zoo

Each box contains one sound but sometimes more than one grapheme. Focus graphemes are **circled***.*

Green words

Read in Fred Talk (pure sounds).

mix	snip	cli<u>ck</u>	clap	spla<u>sh</u>	ca<u>tch</u>
bru<u>sh</u>	text	<u>ch</u>op			

Read the root word first and then with the ending.

hand → hands   <u>thing</u> → <u>thing</u>s

Red words

do   of

Hands

Introduction

*We use our hands every day
for all sorts of things.
How have you used your hands today?
You are using your hands right now
to turn the pages in this book!
Now turn the page to see how else we
use our amazing hands ...*

Written by Gill Munton

Vocabulary check

Discuss the meaning (as used in the non-fiction text) after the children have read the word.

	definition
snip	*to make small cuts with a pair of scissors*
text	*to send a written message using a mobile phone*
pat	*to stroke a pet*

Punctuation to note:

Hands	*Capital letters that start sentences*
.	*Full stop at the end of each sentence*
!	*Exclamation mark*
…	*'Wait and see' dots*

Hands can do lots of things!

Hands can push ...

... and hands can pull.

Hands can dig ...

... and hands can splash!

Hands can snip ...

... and hands can brush.

Hands can click ...

... and hands can text.

Hands can chop ...

... and hands can mix.

Hands can catch ...

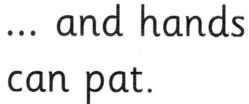

... and hands can pat.

Hands can bang
a drum ...
... and hands
can clap.

Hands can do lots
of things!

Questions to talk about ★ ✶

FIND IT
✓ *Turn to the page*
✓ *Read the question*
✓ *Find the answer*

Page 11:   What can hands do in sand?
Page 12:   What can hands do with scissors?
Page 14:   What can hands do with a spoon?
Page 16:   What can hands bang?

Speed words

Children practise reading the words across the rows, down the columns and in and out of order clearly and quickly.

can	lots	catch	brush	drum
dig	hands	pat	and	chop
pull	clap	mix	splash	bang
snip	push	things	of	text